friendly pho

An Amazing Machine

By Cindy Leaney

Illustrated by Sue King and Peter Wilks

ROURKE CLASSROOM RESOURCES

The path to student success

Note to Parents and Teachers/Educators

Before reading: Ask your child what this book might be about. Read the title aloud together. Then ask what sound the letter *m* makes in *amazing* and *machine*. Then remind your child to listen for that sound in the story.

Written by Cindy Leaney
Designed by Ruth Shane
Illustrated by Sue King & Peter Wilks
Project managed by Gemma Cooper

Created and Designed by SGA and Media Management
18 High Street, Hadleigh, Suffolk, IP7 5AP, U.K.

P. O. Box 3328, Vero Beach
Florida, 32964, U.S.A.
Editor: Patty Whitehouse

Printed in China

ISBN 1-58952-913-8

An Amazing Machine

I'm making the most amazing machine.

In a minute you'll see what I mean.

It mixes marvelous milkshakes–
creamy and thick.

I make it move with one simple flick.

This mobile is like the motor
that makes it start.

The mobile moves the mouse pad.

That's the next part.

The mouse pad bumps the marble and makes it move.

It comes down the middle into this groove.

The marble moves the monster

and makes him push the broom.

Then the broom moves the monkey

and he swings across the room.

The monkey has a magnet and it flips the mixer on.

The main part is over.
Now we're almost done.

I measured the milk and ice cream

and I put in milkshake mix.

Mmmm. This milkshake is creamy,

and it was so simple to fix!

Game time!

Match the words from the story to the pictures!

1. monkey
2. ice cream
3. mobile
4. magnet
5. mouse pad
6. broom

Answers: **1.** e, **2.** f, **3.** c, **4.** d, **5.** b, **6.** a.

Fill in the missing letter *m*s to find new words. What are they?

1. _ arch
2. _ ask
3. _ ore
4. _ ice
5. ti _ e
6. ca _ p

Answers: **1.** march, **2.** mask, **3.** more, **4.** mice, **5.** time, **6.** camp.